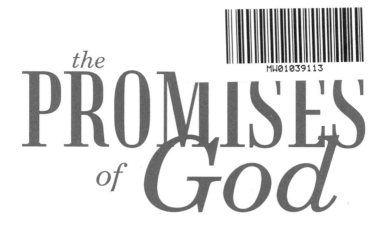

the
PROMISES
of *God*

A Daily
Journal
for Men

A BARBOUR BOOK

All Scripture is from the King James Version.

ISBN 1-55748-775-8—Promises of God
ISBN 1-55748-203-9—My Day

January 1

"Seek ye first the kingdom of God, and his righteousness; and all these things shall be added unto you." MATTHEW 6:33

January 2

"Evening, and morning, and at noon, will I pray, and cry aloud: and he shall hear my voice." PSALM 55:17

January 3

"And whatever ye shall ask in my name, that will I do, that the Father may be glorified in the Son." JOHN 14:13

January 4

"He hath made every thing beautiful in its time: . . ." ECCLESIASTES 3:11

January 5

"Let us hold fast the profession of our faith without wavering (for he is faithful that promised)." HEBREWS 10:23

January 6

"He that handleth a matter wisely shall find good: and whoso trusteth in the Lord, happy is he." PROVERBS 16:20

January 7

"The effectual, fervent prayer of a righteous man availeth much." JAMES 5:16

_____

_____

_____

_____

_____

_____

_____

_____

_____

_____

January 8

"Though your sins be as scarlet, they shall be made white as snow;" ISAIAH 1:18

_____

_____

_____

_____

_____

_____

_____

_____

_____

_____

January 9

"But if we walk in the light, as he is in the light, we have fellowship one with another." 1 JOHN 1:7

January 10

"Every word of God is pure: he is a shield unto them that put their trust in him." PROVERBS 30:5

January 11

"I will never leave thee, nor forsake thee." HEBREWS 13:5

_____

_____

_____

_____

_____

_____

_____

_____

_____

_____

January 12

"The Lord is good, a stronghold in the day of trouble; and he knoweth them that trust in him." NAHUM 1:7

_____

_____

_____

_____

_____

_____

_____

_____

_____

_____

January 13

"But godliness with contentment is great gain." 1 TIMOTHY 6:6

_____

_____

_____

_____

_____

_____

_____

_____

_____

January 14

"For I the Lord thy God will hold thy right hand, saying unto thee, Fear not; I will help thee." ISAIAH 41:13

_____

_____

_____

_____

_____

_____

_____

_____

_____

January 15

"If God be for us, who can be against us?" ROMANS 8:31

_____

_____

_____

_____

_____

_____

_____

_____

_____

January 16

"I will instruct thee and teach thee in the way which thou shalt go." PSALM 32:8

_____

_____

_____

_____

_____

_____

_____

_____

_____

_____

January 17

"For where two or three are gathered together in my name, there am I

January 18

"He shall deliver thee in six troubles: yea, in seven there shall no evil touch thee." JOB 5:19

January 19

"And ye are Christ's; and Christ is God's." 1 CORINTHIANS 3:23

_____

_____

_____

_____

_____

_____

_____

_____

_____

_____

January 20

". . .Behold, I will pour out my spirit unto you, I will make known my words unto you." PROVERBS 1:23

_____

_____

_____

_____

_____

_____

_____

_____

_____

_____

January 21

"Walk in the Spirit, and ye shall not fulfill the lust of the flesh."
GALATIANS 5:16

_____

_____

_____

_____

_____

_____

_____

_____

_____

January 22

"The Lord preserveth all them that love him." PSALM 145:20

_____

_____

_____

_____

_____

_____

_____

_____

_____

_____

January 23

"And let us not be weary in well doing: for in due season we shall reap, if we faint not." GALATIANS 6:9

_____

_____

_____

_____

_____

_____

_____

_____

_____

January 24

"And he shall be like a tree planted by the rivers of water."
PSALM 1:3

_____

_____

_____

_____

_____

_____

_____

_____

_____

_____

January 25

"He that followeth me shall not walk in darkness, but shall have the light of life." JOHN 8:12

January 26

"Fear thou not; for I am with thee." ISAIAH 41:10

January 27

"We are more than conquerors through him that loved us."
ROMANS 8:37

January 28

"The Lord is good unto them that wait for him, to the soul that seeketh him." LAMENTATIONS 3:25

January 29

"To live is Christ, and to die is gain." PHILIPPIANS 1:21

January 30

"The Lord executeth righteousness and judgment for all that are oppressed." PSALM 103:6

January 31

"Greater is he that is in you, than he that is in the world."
1 JOHN 4:4

February 1

"Blessed is the man that trusteth in the Lord, and whose hope the Lord is." JEREMIAH 17:7

February 2

"...And the blood of Jesus Christ his Son cleanseth us from all sin." 1 JOHN 1:7

February 3

"I will guide thee with mine eye." PSALM 32:8

February 4

"Behold, I come quickly." REVELATION 22:7

February 5

"I will strengthen thee; yea, I will help thee; yea, I will uphold thee with the right hand of my righteousness." ISAIAH 41:10

February 6

". . .All things work together for good to them that love God,"
ROMANS 8:28

February 7

"But they that wait upon the Lord shall renew their strength."
ISAIAH 40:31

February 8

"And I give unto them eternal life; and they shall never perish, neither shall any man pluck them out of my hand."
JOHN 10:28

February 9

"The Lord of hosts is with us; the God of Jacob is our refuge." PSALM 46:11

February 10

"He that soweth to the Spirit shall of the Spirit reap life everlasting." GALATIANS 6:8

February 11

"He took not away the pillar of the cloud by day, nor the pillar of fire by night, from before the people." EXODUS 13:22

February 12

"My grace is sufficient for thee: for my strength is made perfect in weakness." 2 CORINTHIANS 12:9

February 13

"I will pour water upon him that is thirsty, and floods upon the dry ground." ISAIAH 44:3

February 14

"...And every one that loveth is born of God, and knoweth God." 1 JOHN 4:7

February 15

"He giveth power to the faint; and to them that have no might he increaseth strength." ISAIAH 40:29

February 16

"Grace and peace be multiplied unto you through the knowledge of God, and of Jesus, our Lord." 2 PETER 1:2

February 17

"Call upon me in the day of trouble: I will deliver thee, and thou shalt glorify Me." PSALM 50:15

February 18

"And being fully persuaded that, what he had promised, he was able also to perform." ROMANS 4:21

February 19

"The Lord shall preserve thee from all evil: He shall preserve thy soul." PSALM 121:7

February 20

"And I will give unto thee the keys of the kingdom of heaven." MATTHEW 16:19

February 21

"Ye shall not be afraid of the face of man; for the judgment is God's." DEUTERONOMY 1:17

February 22

"I will give unto him that is athirst of the fountain of the water of life freely." REVELATION 21:6

February 23

"Those that be planted in the house of the Lord shall flourish in the courts of our God." PSALM 92:13

February 24

"For my yoke is easy, and my burden is light." MATTHEW 11:30

February 25

". . .the Lord will hear when I call unto Him." PSALM 4:3

February 26

"And God is able to make all grace abound toward you,"
2 Corinthians 9:8

February 27

"He shall feed his flock like a shepherd." Isaiah 40:11

February 28

"Come ye after me, and I will make you to become fishers of men." MARK 1:17

_____
_____
_____
_____
_____
_____
_____
_____
_____
_____

February 29

"For thou wilt light my candle: the Lord my God will enlighten my darkness." PSALM 18:28

_____
_____
_____
_____
_____
_____
_____
_____
_____
_____
_____

March 1

"The desire of the righteous shall be granted." PROVERBS 10:24

March 2

"Let us therefore come boldly unto the throne of grace, that we may obtain mercy. . ." HEBREWS 4:16

March 3

"The young lions do lack, and suffer hunger: but they that seek the Lord shall not want any good thing." PSALM 34:10

March 4

". . .Thy Father which seeth in secret himself shall reward thee openly." MATTHEW 6:4

March 5

"Though our outward man perish, yet the inward man is renewed day by day." 2 CORINTHIANS 4:16

March 6

". . .He that dwelleth in love dwelleth in God, and God in him." 1 JOHN 4:16

March 7

"I will be with him in trouble; I will deliver him, and honor him." PSALM 91:15

March 8

"For our light affliction, which is but for a moment, worketh for us a far more exceeding and eternal weight of glory."
2 CORINTHIANS 4:17

March 9

"Great is thy faithfulness." LAMENTATIONS 3:23

March 10

"Above all, taking the shield of faith, wherewith ye shall be able to quench all the fiery darts of the wicked."
EPHESIANS 6:16

March 11

"Hath he said, and shall he not do it? or hath He spoken, and shall He not make it good?" NUMBERS 23:19

March 12

"Behold, I show you a mystery; We shall not all sleep, but we sleep, but we shall all be changed." 1 CORINTHIANS 15:51

March 13

"Then will I hear from heaven, and will forgive their sin, and will heal their land." 2 CHRONICLES 7:14

March 14

"And there shall be no night there. . .for the Lord God giveth them light: and they shall reign forever and ever."
REVELATIONS 22:5

March 15

"The Lord is nigh unto all them that call upon Him, to all that call upon Him in truth." PSALM 145:18

March 16

"And as we have borne the image of the earthy, we shall also bear the image of the heavenly." 1 CORINTHIANS 15:49

March 17

"My defense is of God, which saveth the upright in heart."
PSALM 7:10

March 18

"He that loveth his brother abideth in the light." 1 JOHN 2:10

March 19

"The Lord shall preserve thy going out and thy coming in from this time forth and even for evermore." PSALM 121:8

March 20

"For in that He Himself hath suffered being tempted, He is able to succour them that are tempted." HEBREWS 2:18

March 21

"And ye shall seek Me, and find Me, when ye shall search for Me with all your heart." JEREMIAH 29:13

March 22

"For whosoever shall call upon the name of the Lord shall be saved." ROMANS 10:13

March 23

"He will not suffer thy foot to be moved: He that keepeth thee will not slumber." PSALM 121:3

March 24

"For God hath not appointed us to wrath, but to obtain salvation by our Lord Jesus Christ." 1 THESSALONIANS 5:9

March 25

"...my kindness shall not depart from thee...saith the Lord, that hath mercy on thee." ISAIAH 54:10

March 26

"And this I pray, that your love may abound yet more and more in knowledge and in all judgment." PHILIPPIANS 1:9

March 27

"I will dwell in the midst of thee." ZECHARIAH 2:11

March 28

"Blessed are the pure in heart: for they shall see God."
MATTHEW 5:8

March 29

"Commit thy way unto the Lord; trust also in him; and he shall bring it to pass." PSALM 37:5

March 30

"The Spirit itself beareth witness with our spirit, that we are the children of God." ROMANS 8:16

March 31

"I will even make a way in the wilderness, and rivers in the desert." ISAIAH 43:19

_____

_____

_____

_____

_____

_____

_____

_____

_____

April 1

"For the Lord Himself shall descend from heaven with a shout. . .and the dead in Christ shall rise first." 1 THESSALONIANS 4:16

_____

_____

_____

_____

_____

_____

_____

_____

_____

April 2

"He shall call upon Me and I will answer him. . ."
PSALM 91:15

April 3

"I am the resurrection, and the Life: he that believeth in Me,
though he were dead, yet shall he live." JOHN 11:25

April 4

"Call unto me, and I will answer thee, and show thee great and mighty things." JEREMIAH 33:3

April 5

"Now thanks be unto God, which always causeth us to triumph

April 6

"I will bless the Lord, who hath given me counsel." PSALM 16:7

_____

_____

_____

_____

_____

_____

_____

_____

_____

_____

_____

April 7

"For the eyes of the Lord are over the righteous and His ears are open unto their prayers." 1 PETER 3:12

_____

_____

_____

_____

_____

_____

_____

_____

_____

_____

_____

April 8

"No weapon that is formed against thee shall prosper."
ISAIAH 54:17

April 9

"For God so loved the world, that he gave his only begotten Son, that whosoever believeth in him should. . .have everlasting life." JOHN 3:16

April 10

"Blessed are they that keep his testimonies, and that seek Him with the whole heart." PSALM 119:2

April 11

"Blessed are the peacemakers: for they shall be called the children of God." MATTHEW 5:9

April 12

"But if from thence thou shalt seek the Lord thy God, thou shalt find Him.." DEUTERONOMY 4:29

April 13

"So then faith cometh by hearing, and hearing by the word of God." ROMANS 10:17

April 14

"Weeping may endure for a night, but joy cometh in the morning." PSALM 30:5

April 15

"For if our heart condemn us, God is greater than our heart, and knoweth all things. . ." 1 JOHN 3:20

April 16

"I send an Angel before thee, to keep thee in the way, and to bring thee into the place which I have prepared."
EXODUS 23:20

April 17

"Every good gift and every perfect gift is from above, and cometh down from the Father of lights." JAMES 1:17

April 18

"For them that honor me I will honor. . ." 1 SAMUEL 2:30

April 19

"For the word of God is quick, and powerful, and sharper than any twoedged sword." HEBREWS 4:12

April 20

"As for God, His way is perfect." PSALM 18:30

April 21

"And you hath he quickened, who were dead in trespasses and sins;. . ." EPHESIANS 2:1

April 22

"Understand therefore this day, that the Lord thy God is He which goeth over before thee;" DEUTERONOMY 9:3

April 23

"For God hath not given us the spirit of fear; but of power, and of love, and of a sound mind." 2 TIMOTHY 1:7

April 24

"I will ransom them from the power of the grave; I will redeem them from death." HOSEA 13:14

April 25

"For we are His workmanship, created in Christ Jesus unto good works." EPHESIANS 2:10

April 26

"I will seek that which was lost, and bring again that which was driven away." EZEKIEL 34:16

_____

_____

_____

_____

_____

_____

_____

_____

_____

_____

April 27

"Casting all your care upon Him; for He careth for you." 1 PETER 5:7

_____

_____

_____

_____

_____

_____

_____

_____

_____

_____

April 28

"Thy word have I hid in my heart, that I might not sin against thee." PSALM 119:11

_____

_____

_____

_____

_____

_____

_____

_____

_____

_____

April 29

"If any of you lack wisdom, let him ask of God, that giveth to all men liberally." JAMES 1:5

_____

_____

_____

_____

_____

_____

_____

_____

_____

_____

_____

April 30

"Sorrow is turned into joy before him." JOB 41:22

_____

May 1

"As I was with Moses, so I will be with thee; I will not fail thee, nor forsake thee." JOSHUA 1:5

May 2

"But my God shall supply all your need according to his riches in glory by Christ Jesus." PHILIPPIANS 4:19

May 3

"Thou wilt keep him in perfect peace, whose mind is stayed on thee. . ." ISAIAH 26:3

May 4

"And when the chief Shepherd shall appear, ye shall receive a crown of glory that fadeth not away." 1 PETER 5:4

May 5

"The Lord will perfect that which concerneth me: Thy mercy, O Lord, endureth for ever." PSALM 138:8

May 6

"If we confess our sins, he is faithful and just to forgive us our sins," 1 JOHN 1:9

May 7

"And I will give peace in the land, and ye shall lie down, and none shall make you afraid." LEVITICUS 26:6

May 8

"For by grace are ye saved through faith;" EPHESIANS 2:8

May 9

"Wait on the Lord: be of good courage, and He shall strengthen thine heart." PSALM 27:14

May 10

"He that findeth his life shall lose it: and he that loseth his life for My sake shall find it." MATTHEW 10:39

May 11

"And this is the record, that God hath given to us eternal life, and this life is in His Son." 1 JOHN 5:11

May 12

". . .Thou shalt compass me about with songs of deliverance." PSALM 32:7

May 13

"Now unto Him that is able to keep you from falling, and to present you faultless before the presence of His glory with exceeding joy," JUDE 1:24

May 14

"For I know the thoughts that I think toward you, saith the Lord, thoughts of peace, and not of evil. . ." JEREMIAH 29:11

May 15

". . .For God cannot be tempted with evil, neither tempteth He any man. . ." JAMES 1:13

May 16

"I sought the Lord, and He heard me, and delivered me from all my fears." PSALM 34:4

May 17

"Nor height, nor depth, nor any other creature, shall be able to separate us from the love of God. . ." ROMANS 8:39

May 18

"For the Lord thy God bringeth thee into a good land."
DEUTERONOMY 8:7

May 19

"Love never faileth." 1 CORINTHIANS 13:8

May 20

". . .For whither thou goest, I will go; and where thou lodgest, I will lodge: thy people shall be my people, and thy God my God." RUTH 1:16

May 21

"For Christ is the end of the law for righeousness to every one that believeth." ROMANS 10:4

May 22

"And ye shall serve the Lord your God, and He shall bless thy bread, and thy water;" Exodus 23:25

May 23

"Your sorrow shall be turned into joy." John 16:20

May 24

"He will keep the feet of his saints. . ." 1 SAMUEL 2:9

May 25

"The sufferings of the present time are not worthy to be compared with the glory which shall be revealed in us." ROMANS 8:18

May 26

"Better is little with the fear of the Lord than great treasure and trouble therewith." PROVERBS 15:16

May 27

"All scripture is given by inspiration of God and is profitable." 2 TIMOTHY 3:16

May 28

"Thou art my hiding place; thou shalt preserve me from trouble. . ." PSALM 32:7

May 29

"There is therefore now no condemnation to them which are in Christ Jesus." ROMANS 8:1

May 30

"But whoso hearkeneth unto me shall dwell safely, and shall be quiet from fear of evil." PROVERBS 1:33

May 31

". . .Eye hath not seen, nor ear heard. . .the things which God hath prepared for them that love Him." 1 CORINTHIANS 2:9

June 1

"Draw nigh to God, and He will draw nigh to you." JAMES 4:8

June 2

"The grass withereth, the flower fadeth: but the word of our God shall stand for ever." ISAIAH 40:8

June 3

"Nevertheless we, according to His promise, look for new heavens and a new earth, wherein dwelleth righteousness."
2 PETER 3:13

June 4

"Through God we shall do valiantly." PSALM 60:12

June 5

". . .For we have heard Him ourselves, and know that this is indeed the Christ, the Saviour of the world." JOHN 4:42

June 6

". . .The hand of our God is upon all them for good that seek him." EZRA 8:22

June 7

"Rejoice, because your names are written in heaven."
LUKE 10:20

June 8

". . .Be not afraid, neither be thou dismayed: for the Lord thy God is with thee withersoever thou goest." JOSHUA 1:9

June 9

"But ye shall receive power, after the Holy Ghost is come upon you;" ACTS 1:8

_____

_____

_____

_____

_____

_____

_____

_____

_____

_____

June 10

"The Lord, before whom I walk, will send His angel with thee, and prosper thy way;." GENESIS 24:40

_____

_____

_____

_____

_____

_____

_____

_____

_____

_____

June 11

". . .Being justified by faith, we have peace with God through our Lord Jesus Christ." ROMANS 5:1

June 12

"Delight thyself also in the Lord; and He shall give thee the desires of thine heart." PSALM 37:4

June 13

"When Christ, who is our life, shall appear, then shall ye also appear with Him in glory." COLOSSIANS 3:4

June 14

"The Lord He is God in heaven above, and upon the earth beneath; there is none else," DEUTERONOMY 4:39

June 15

"In Christ shall all be made alive" 1 Corinthians 15:22

_____

_____

_____

_____

_____

_____

_____

_____

_____

_____

June 16

"Many are the afflictions of the righteous: but the Lord delivereth him out of them all." Psalm 34:19

_____

_____

_____

_____

_____

_____

_____

_____

_____

_____

June 17

"With men it is impossible, but not with God: for with God all things are possible." MARK 10:27

June 18

"And all thy children shall be taught of the Lord; and great shall be the peace of thy children." ISAIAH 54:13

June 19

"The Lord knoweth how to deliver the godly out of temptations." 2 PETER 2:9

_____
_____
_____
_____
_____
_____
_____
_____
_____
_____

June 20

"Thou shalt make thy prayer unto him, and he shall hear thee. . ." JOB 22:27

_____
_____
_____
_____
_____
_____
_____
_____
_____
_____

June 21

"It is your Father's good pleasure to give you the kingdom."
LUKE 12:32

June 22

"I will make the wilderness a pool of water, and the dry land springs of water." ISAIAH 41:18

June 23

"Henceforth there is laid up for me a crown of righteousness, which the Lord, the righteous judge, shall give me at that day." 2 TIMOTHY 4:8

June 24

"Thy word is a lamp unto my feet, and a light unto my path." PSALM 119:105

June 25

"He being not a forgetful hearer, but a doer of the work, this man shall be blessed in his deed.." JAMES 1:25

June 26

". . .Yet will he have compassion according to the multitude of his mercies." LAMENTATIONS 3:32

June 27

"He that is begotten of God keepeth himself, and that wicked one toucheth him not." 1 JOHN 5:18

June 28

"The Lord is long suffering, and of great mercy, forgiving iniquity and transgression." NUMBERS 14:18

June 29

"For all the law is fulfilled in one word, even in this; thou shalt love thy neighbor as thyself." GALATIANS 5:14

June 30

"Be still, and know that I am God." PSALM 46:10

July 1

"A good man obtaineth favor of the Lord." PROVERBS 12:2

July 2

". . .To an inheritance incorruptible, and undefiled, and that fadeth not away, reserved in heaven for you." 1 PETER 1:4

July 3

"To him that soweth righteousness shall be a sure reward."
PROVERBS 11:18

July 4

"And the peace of God, which passeth all understanding,
shall keep your hearts and minds through Christ Jesus."
PHILIPPIANS 4:7

July 5

"For I will forgive their iniquity, and I will remember their sin no more." JEREMIAH 31:34

July 6

"But God is faithful, who will not suffer you to be tempted above that ye are able;" 1 CORINTHIANS 10:13

July 7

"For the Lord your God is gracious and merciful, and will not turn away his face from you, if ye return unto him."
2 CHRONICLES 30:9

July 8

"But the God of all grace. . .after that ye have suffered a while, make you perfect, stablish, strengthen, settle you."
1 PETER 5:10

July 9

"The steps of a good man are ordered by the Lord: and He delighteth in his way." PSALM 37:23

July 10

"And the fruit of righteousness is sown in peace by them that make peace." JAMES 3:18

July 11

"Then shalt thou call, and the Lord shall answer." ISAIAH 58:9

July 12

"Blessed is the man that endureth temptation: for when he is tried, he shall receive the crown of life. . ." JAMES 1:12

July 13

". . .A God ready to pardon, gracious and merciful, slow to anger, and of great kindness. . ." NEHEMIAH 9:17

July 14

"Ye are all the children of light, and the children of the day." 1 THESSALONIANS 5:5

July 15

"But as truly as I live, all the earth shall be filled with the glory of the Lord." NUMBERS 14:21

July 16

"But if ye be led of the Spirit, ye are nut under the law." GALATIANS 5:18

July 17

"A soft answer turneth away wrath. . ." PROVERBS 15:1

July 18

"The Lord is not slack concerning His promise." 2 PETER 3:9

July 19

"I, even I, am He that comforteth you. . ." ISAIAH 51:12

July 20

"If ye abide in me, and my words abide in you, ye shall ask what ye will, and it shall be done unto you." JOHN 15:7

July 21

"For I have satiated the weary soul, and I have replenished every sorrowful soul." JEREMIAH 31:25

July 22

"Ye are God's husbandry, ye are God's building."
1 CORINTHIANS 3:9

July 23

"And the Lord shall guide thee continually, and satisfy thy soul in drought." ISAIAH 58:11

July 24

"Being filled with the fruits of righteousness, which are by Jesus Christ, unto the glory and praise of God."
PHILIPPIANS 1:11

July 25

"Whoso offereth praise glorifieth me." PSALM 50:23

July 26

"We. . .do notcease to pray for you, and to desire that ye might be filled with the knowledge of His will. . ."
COLOSSIANS 1:9

July 27

"How precious also are thy thoughts unto me, O God! How great is the sum of them!" PSALM 139:17

July 28

". . .For ye are all one in Christ Jesus." GALATIANS 3:28

July 29

"The Lord your God hath given you rest, and hath given you this land." JOSHUA 1:13

July 30

"Blessed be the God and Father of our Lord Jesus Christ, who hath blessed us with all spiritual blessings in heavenly places." EPHESIANS 1:3

July 31

"Acquaint now thyself with Him, and be at peace: thereby good shall come unto thee." JOB 22:21

August 1

"And he said, My presence shall go with thee, and I will give thee rest." EXODUS 33:14

August 2

"He that hath the Son hath life. . ." 1 JOHN 5:12

August 3

"The fear of the Lord prolongeth days. . ." PROVERBS 10:27

August 4

"According as his divine power hath given unto us all things that pertain unto life and godliness." 2 PETER 1:3

August 5

"The Lord lift up his countenance upon thee, and give thee peace." NUMBERS 6:26

August 6

"Verily, verily, I say unto you, if a man keep My saying, he shall never see death." JOHN 8:51

August 7

"And I have put my words in thy mouth, and I have covered thee in the shadow of mine hand." ISAIAH 51:16

August 8

"Submit yourselves therefore to God. Resist the devil, and he will flee from you." JAMES 4:7

_____

_____

_____

_____

_____

_____

_____

_____

_____

August 9

". . .To him that ordereth his conversation aright will I show the salvation of God." PSALM 50:23

_____

_____

_____

_____

_____

_____

_____

_____

_____

August 10

".. .For blessed are they who keep my ways." PROVERBS 8:32

August 11

"And he believed in the Lord; and he counted it to him for righteousness." GENESIS 15:6

August 12

"For there is one God, and one mediator between God and men, the man Christ Jesus;" 1 TIMOTHY 2:5

August 13

"For the Lord your God is he who hath fought for you."
JOSHUA 23:3

August 14

"For this corruptible must put on incorruption, and this mortal must put on immortality." 1 CORINTHIANS 15:53

August 15

"The Lord preserveth the faithful." PSALM 31:23

August 16

"The words that I speak unto you, they are spirit, and they are life." JOHN 6:63

August 17

"For the Lord God will help me; therefore shall I not be confounded." ISAIAH 50:7

August 18

"What things soever ye desire, when ye pray, believe that ye receive them, and ye shall have them." MARK 11:24

August 19

"And He shall bring forth thy righteousness as the light, and thy judgment as the noonday." PSALM 37:6

August 20

"The gift of God is eternal life." ROMANS 6:23

August 21

"He hath remembered his covenant for ever, the word which he commanded to a thousand generations." PSALM 105:8

August 22

"But as many as received him, to them gave he power to become the sons of God," JOHN 1:12

_____
_____
_____
_____
_____
_____
_____
_____
_____

August 23

"He healeth the broken in heart, and bindeth up their wounds." PSALM 147:3

_____
_____
_____
_____
_____
_____
_____
_____
_____
_____

August 24

"I the Lord have called thee in righteousness, and will hold thine hand, and will keep thee. . ." ISAIAH 42:6

August 25

"Therefore if any man be in Christ, he is a new creature: old things are passed away; behold, all things are become new." 2 CORINTHIANS 5:17

August 26

"And it shall come to pass afterward, that I will pour out my spirit upon all flesh;. . ." JOEL 2:28

August 27

"Because thou hast kept the word of my patience, I also will keep thee from the hour of temptation." REVELATION 3:10

August 28

"Fear thou not; for I am with thee: be not dismayed; for I am thy God." ISAIAH 41:10

August 29

"And whosoever liveth and believeth in Me shall never die." JOHN 11:26

August 30

"For I am the Lord, I change not;. . ." MALACHI 3:6

August 31

"For ye are all the children of God by faith in Christ Jesus."
GALATIANS 3:26

September 1

"And I will take sickness away from the midst of thee."
EXODUS 23:25

September 2

"Blessed are the merciful: for they shall obtain mercy."
MATTHEW 5:7

September 3

"Though I walk in the midst of trouble, thou wilt revive me:"
PSALM 138:7

September 4

"For whatsoever is born of God overcometh the world."
1 JOHN 5:4

September 5

"Commit thy works unto the Lord, and thy thoughts shall be established." PROVERBS 16:3

September 6

"But by the grace of God I am what I am." 1 CORINTHIANS 15:10

September 7

"Then they that feared the Lord spake often one to another: and the Lord hearkened, and heard it." MALACHI 3:16

September 8

"Stand fast therefore in the liberty wherewith Christ hath made us free," GALATIANS 5:1

September 9

". . .I have broken the bands of your yoke, and made you go upright." LEVITICUS 26:13

September 10

"And account that the longsuffering of our Lord is salvation." 2 PETER 3:15

September 11

"Though he fall, he shall not be utterly cast down: for the Lord upholdeth him with his hand." PSALM 37:24

September 12

"For the Son of man is not come to destroy men's lives, but to save them." LUKE 9:56

September 13

"There failed not aught of any good thing which the Lord had spoken unto the house of Israel; all came to pass."
JOSHUA 21:45

September 14

"Humble yourselves in the sight of the Lord, and He shall lift you up." JAMES 4:10

September 15

"I love them that love me; and those that seek me early shall find me." PROVERBS 8:17

September 16

"The word of the Lord endureth forever." 1 Peter 1:25

September 17

"I will heal their backsliding, I will love them freely." HOSEA 14:4

September 18

"Behold, I stand at the door, and knock: if any man hear My voice, and open the door, I will come in. . . ." REVELATION 3:20

September 19

"I am the Lord your God, and none else: and my people shall never be ashamed." JOEL 2:27

September 20

"Wherefore thou art no more a servant, but a son; and if a son, then an heir of God through Christ." GALATIANS 4:7

September 21

"For ye shall not go out with haste, nor go by flight: for the Lord shall go before you." ISAIAH 52:12

September 22

"Faithful is He that calleth you, who also will do it." 1 THESSALONIANS 5:24

September 23

"But the salvation of the righteous is of the Lord: He is their strength in the time of trouble." PSALM 37:39

September 24

"He which soweth bountifully shall reap also bountifully."
2 CORINTHIANS 9:6

September 25

"He that giveth unto the poor shall not lack. . . ."
PROVERBS 28:27

September 26

"For this purpose the Son of God was manifested, that He might destroy the works of the devil." 1 JOHN 3:8

September 27

"Fear not. . .I am thy shield, and thy exceeding great reward." GENESIS 15:1

September 28

"Ask, and it shall be given you; seek, and ye shall find; kock, and it shall be opened unto you." MATTHEW 7:7

September 29

"They that sow in tears shall reap in joy." PSALM 126:5

September 30

"Believe on the Lord Jesus Christ, and thou shalt be saved, and thy house.." ACTS 16:31

October 1

"Cast thy burden upon the Lord, and He shall sustain thee: He shall never suffer the righteous to be moved."
PSALM 55:22

October 2

"And all things, whatsoever ye shall ask in prayer, believing, ye shall receive." MATTHEW 21:22

October 3

"I know that thou canst do every thing, and that no thought can be withholden from thee" JOB 42:2

October 4

". . .He which hath begun a good work in you will perform it until the day of Jesus Christ." PHILIPPIANS 1:6

October 5

"He that hath pity upon the poor lendeth unto the Lord; and that which he hath given will He pay him again."
PROVERBS 19:17

October 6

"The just shall live by faith." GALATIANS 3:11

October 7

"I do set My bow in the cloud, and it shall be for a token of a covenant between me and the earth." GENESIS 9:13

October 8

"Now the Lord is that Spirit: and where the Spirit of the Lord is, there is liberty." 2 CORINTHIANS 3:17

October 9

"The Lord thy God in the midst of thee is mighty; He will save, He will rejoice over thee with joy;" ZEPHANIAH 3:17

October 10

"For we know that if our earthly house of this tabernacle were dissolved, we have a building of God, . . .eternal in the heavens." 2 CORINTHIANS 5:1

October 11

"Behold, I am the Lord, the God of all flesh: is there any thing too hard for Me?" JEREMIAH 32:27

October 12

"I am come a light into the world, that whosoever believeth on me should not abide in darkness." JOHN 12:46

October 13

"The angel of the Lord encampeth round about them that fear Him, and delivereth them." PSALM 34:7

October 14

"In the world ye shall have tribulation: but be of good cheer; I have overcome the world." JOHN 16:33

October 15

"And when I see the blood, I will pass over you, and the plague shall not be upon you to destroy you." EXODUS 12:13

_____

_____

_____

_____

_____

_____

_____

_____

_____

_____

October 16

"If any man will do His will, he shall know of the doctrine." JOHN 7:17

_____

_____

_____

_____

_____

_____

_____

_____

_____

_____

October 17

"Surely I will be with thee." JUDGES 6:16

October 18

"Blessed are they that mourn: for they shall be comforted."
MATTHEW 5:4

October 19

"When thou walkest through the fire, thou shalt not be burned; neither shall the flame kindle upon thee." Isaiah 43:2

October 20

"Take no thought how or what ye shall speak: for it shall be given you in that same hour what ye shall speak." Matthew 10:19

October 21

"By humility and the fear of the Lord are riches, and honor, and life." PROVERBS 22:4

_____

October 22

"To him that overcometh will I give to eat of the hidden manna," REVELATION 2:17

_____

October 23

"For as the heaven is high above the earth, so great is his mercy toward them that fear him." PSALM 103:11

October 24

"But thanks be to God, which giveth us the victory through our Lord Jesus Christ." 1 CORINTHIANS 15:57

October 25

"And it shall come to pass, that whosoever shall call on the name of the Lord shall be delivered." JOEL 2:32

October 26

"For God is not the author of confusion, but of peace. . . ." 1 CORINTHIANS 14:33

October 27

". . .I will look unto the Lord; I will wait for the God of my salvation: my God will hear me." MICAH 7:7

October 28

"But where sin abounded, grace did much more abound." ROMANS 5:20

October 29

"But unto you that fear my name shall the Sun of righeousness arise with healing in his wings. . ." MALACHI 4:2

October 30

"Peace I leave with you, My peace I give unto you: not as the
world giveth, give I unto you." JOHN 14:27

October 31

"It is God that girdeth me with strength, and maketh my way perfect." PSALM 18:32

November 1

"The Lord is on my side; I will not fear: what can man do unto me?" PSALM 118:6

November 2

"Jesus saith unto him, I am the way, the truth, and the life: no man cometh unto me Father, but by me." JOHN 14:6

November 3

"And I will walk among you, and will be your God, and ye shall be my people." LEVITICUS 26:12

November 4

"For ye are all the children of God by faith in Christ Jesus."
GALATIANS 3:26

November 5

"God shall send forth his mercy and his truth." PSALM 57:3

November 6

"Who is he that overcometh the world, but he that believeth that Jesus is the Son of God?" 1 JOHN 5:5

November 7

"Behold, the Lord's hand is not shortened, that it cannot save; neither His ear heavy, that it cannot hear." ISAIAH 59:1

November 8

"And such trust have we through Christ to God-ward. . ."
2 CORINTHIANS 3:4

November 9

". . .For the Lord your God, he it is that fighteth for you, as he hath promised you." JOSHUA 23:10

November 10

"Come unto me, all ye that labor and are heavy laden, and I will give you rest." MATTHEW 11:28

November 11

"A thousand shall fall at thy side, and ten thousand at thy right hand; but it shall not come nigh thee." PSALM 91:7

November 12

"He that overcometh, the same shall be clothed in white raiment; and I will not blot out his name out of the book of life." REVELATION 3:5

November 13

"I will command my blessing upon you." LEVITICUS 25:21

November 14

"I indeed have baptized you with water: but He shall baptize you with the Holy Ghost." MARK 1:8

November 15

"For the Lord shall be thy confidence, and shall keep thy foot from being taken." PROVERBS 3:26

November 16

"And God shall wipe away all tears from their eyes; and there shall be no more death." REVELATION 21:4

November 17

". . .My kindness shall not depart from thee. . .saith the Lord who hath mercy on thee" ISAIAH 54:10

November 18

"Know ye not that ye are the temple of God, and that the Spirit of God dwelleth in you?" 1 CORINTHIANS 3:16

November 19

"Great peace have they who love thy law: and nothing shall offend them." PSALM 119:165

November 20

"And ye shall know the truth, and the truth shall make you free." JOHN 8:32

November 21

"And the Lord shall help them, and deliver them: he shall deliver them from the wicked, and save them, because they trust in him." PSALM 37:40

November 22

"Lo, I am with you always, even unto the end of the world."
MATTHEW 28:20

November 23

"Trust in the Lord, and do good; so shalt thou dwell in the land, and verily thou shalt be fed." PSALM 37:3

November 24

"Said I not unto thee that, if thou wouldest believe, thou shouldest see the glory of God?" JOHN 11:40

November 25

"He maketh my feet like hinds' feet, and setteth me upon my high places." PSALM 18:33

November 26

"For the gifts and calling of God are without repentance."
ROMANS 11:29

November 27

"For He shall give His angels charge over thee, to keep thee in all thy ways" PSALM 91:11

November 28

"The Lord shall deliver me from every evil work, and will preserve me unto His Heavenly Kingdom." 2 TIMOTHY 4:18

November 29

"Hitherto hath the Lord helped us" 1 SAMUEL 7:12

November 30

"The God of peace shall be with you." PHILIPPIANS 4:9

_____

_____

_____

_____

_____

_____

_____

_____

_____

December 1

"God sent his only begotten Son into the world, that we might live through him." 1 JOHN 4:9

_____

_____

_____

_____

_____

_____

_____

_____

_____

_____

December 2

"It is of the Lord's mercies that we are not consumed, because his compassions fail not." LAMENTATIONS 3:22

December 3

"For ye were sometimes darknes, but now are ye light in the Lord." EPHESIANS 5:8

December 4

"The Lord is the strength of my life;" PSALM 27:1

_____

_____

_____

_____

_____

_____

_____

_____

_____

_____

December 5

"Give, and it shall be given unto you;" LUKE 6:38

_____

_____

_____

_____

_____

_____

_____

_____

_____

_____

December 6

"The meek shall inherit the earth, and shall delight themselves in the abundance of peace." PSALM 37:11

December 7

"For as many as are led by the Spirit of God, they are the sons of God." ROMANS 8:14

December 8

"The eternal God is thy refuge." DEUTERONOMY 33:27

December 9

"Jesus Christ, the same yesterday, and today, and forever."
HEBREWS 13:8

December 10

"His kingdom is an everlasting kingdom, and his dominion is from generation to generation." DANIEL 4:3

December 11

"For true and righteous are his judgments." REVELATION 19:2

December 12

"For the Lord giveth wisdom: out of his mouth cometh knowledge and understanding." PROVERBS 2:6

December 13

"I can do all things through Christ, which strengtheneth me." PHILIPPIANS 4:13

December 14

"He that believeth and is baptized shall be saved;"
MARK 16:16

_____

_____

_____

_____

_____

_____

_____

_____

_____

December 15

"If ye be willing and obedient, ye shall eat the good of the
land." ISAIAH 1:19

_____

_____

_____

_____

_____

_____

_____

_____

_____

December 16

"Blessed is he that readeth. . .and keeps those things which are written therein: for the time is at hand." REVELATION 1:3

December 17

"And blessed is he, whosoever shall not be offended in me." LUKE 7:23

December 18

"The upright shall dwell in thy presence." PSALM 140:13

December 19

"But the Lord is faithful, who shall stablish you, and keep you from evil." 2 THESSALONIANS 3:3

December 20

"Our God shall fight for us." NEHEMIAH 4:20

December 21

"Blessed are they that hear the word of God, and keep it."
LUKE 11:28

December 22

"Some trust in chariots, and some in horses: but we will remember the name of the Lord our God." PSALM 20:7

December 23

"But unto every one of us is given grace according to the measure of the gift of Christ." EPHESIANS 4:7

December 24

"For unto us a child is born, unto us a son is given."
ISAIAH 9:6

_____

_____

_____

_____

_____

_____

_____

_____

_____

December 25

"I am come that they might have life." JOHN 10:10

_____

_____

_____

_____

_____

_____

_____

_____

_____

_____

December 26

"The Lord thy God, he it is who doth go with thee; he will not fail thee, nor forsake thee." DEUTERONOMY 31:6

December 27

"For with God nothing shall be impossible." LUKE 1:37

December 28

"He shall cover thee with his feathers, and under his wings shalt thou trust: his truth shall be thy shield and buckler."
PSALM 91:4

December 29

"If thou canst believe, all things are possible to him that believeth." MARK 9:23

December 30

"In all thy ways acknowledge him, and he shall direct thy paths." PROVERBS 3:6

December 31

"Allelujah! For the Lord God omnipotent reigneth." REVELATION 19:6